Advance praise for *The Silverback Gorilla Syndrome*

"*The Silverback Gorilla Syndrome* provides a shining mirror for us men to see ourselves more clearly. Hood has hit the male dominance nail on the head. What is more, he offers provocative examples of how we can channel our primitive urges for our own benefit and the world's relief."

Louis Krupnick
Author of *From Despair to Decision*

"I think people need to stop and look at things differently today as we try to reinvent our organizations and ourselves. Jeff Hood gives us a fun and insightful look at how to let go of the power game and play the joy game."

Larry Wilson
Founder of Wilson Learning Corporation and Pecos River/AON Consulting
Author of *Changing the Game* and *Play to Win*

"I love this book! Jeff Hood invites us to look at men's unspoken pain, then embrace the wildman as we step into a whole new world becoming more complex integrated men. It teaches the essential message of all the New Warrior work for men, guiding the journey from the obsolete (old warrior) paradigm of dominance and control into the emerging (New Warrior) paradigm of letting go and trusting. Fear versus love is presented in this beautiful welcome-the-shadow story. Here we see what the new integration feels like, looks like, and acts like as we move toward a new magnificence."

Bill Kauth
Cofounder of the New Warrior Training
Author of *A Circle of Men: The Original Manual for Men's Support Groups*

"This book is must reading for anyone working in men's issues and concerned about helping to heal the violence among us."

Victor LaCerva, MD
Author of *Pathways to Peace: Forty Steps to a Less Violent America*

"Jeff Hood and Jack Lindstrom have produced a wise and witty book. This gorilla enjoyed both the words and the pictures, and I urge my fellow gorillas to try it."

Asa Baber
MEN columnist, *Playboy* Magazine

THE SILVERBACK GORILLA SYNDROME

Robert

One of my favourite

Gorillas.

love

Jeff

THE SILVERBACK GORILLA SYNDROME

Transforming Primitive Man

Written by Jeff Hood

Illustrated by Jack Lindstrom

Adventures in Spirit Publications
Santa Fe, New Mexico

Published by: **Adventures in Spirit Publications**
PO Box 6096
Santa Fe, NM 87502

Edited by Ellen Kleiner
Book design by Richard Harris
Cover design by Janice St. Marie

A Blessingway book

Printed in the United States of America with soy ink on acid-free recycled paper

Publisher's Cataloging-in-Publication Data

Hood, Jeff.
    The silverback gorilla syndrome : transforming primitive man / written by Jeff Hood ; illustrated by Jack Lindstrom -- 1st ed.
    p. cm.
    LCCN: 98-93437
    ISBN: 0-9666147-0-4

    1. Masculinity. 2. Masculinity--Humor. 3. Men--Psychology. 4. Dominance (Psychology) I. Lindstrom, Jack. II. Title.

BF692.5.H66 1999   155.3'32
                    QB198-1507

10 9 8 7 6 5 4 3 2 1

This book is dedicated to my dad,
for showing me how gentle a gorilla could be;
to my mom, for asking the hard questions;
and to my son, in anticipation of a world
that will receive him as a compassionate man.

Acknowledgments

I gratefully acknowledge the following people for their inspiration and enthusiasm along the way: Jonna Lemes for identifying the questions, Bill Proudman for lighting a fire under my butt, Brandt Morgan for being the first to say, "Damn, I wish I'd written that," Ellen Kleiner for patiently dotting my *i*'s and deleting this and that, Michael Hamilton for persisting when my gorilla answered, "No, I don't need any help!" Bill Kauth for calling me back with gusto, and my dog, Kodi, for being such a stud.

I trust this work will not lead to a rash of anti-gorilla sentiment. I apologize to Dian Fossey and the National Geographic Society for any inaccuracies about the noble beasts, who I'm sure have enough troubles of their own.

Gorillas go through life in their communities pretty much the way we do in ours—eating, having sex, raising the young, playing out social roles, getting old, and dying. They can be deeply caring toward one another, especially toward the youngsters. They can also be quite bloodthirsty while competing for territory or status.

Like most social animals, gorillas maintain a hierarchy within the clan. Invariably, a mature male grows a particularly beautiful coat of silver fur on his back, identifying him as the leader. This silverback gorilla takes on the task of preserving the clan: he directs their movement through the forest, sires the offspring, mediates disputes, and defends the clan against threats to their well-being. Ruler of the roost, he enjoys both the privileges and burdens of his position. Other members of the clan organize themselves in subordinate positions, forming a social structure that works well for them. Thousands of years of evolution have proven it to be so.

Evolution for the human race, however, has taken a funny twist. In the course of emerging from the jungles of our primate ancestors, we have stumbled onto, some would say earned, a thing called awareness. This faculty has spawned a body of knowledge leading to science, industry, technology—and ultimately increased comfort and longer lives. But it has also sparked an illusion of separation from the rest of the animal kingdom. Forging ahead in the quest for control over our destiny and our planet, we act as if the laws of nature do not apply to us. We are blind to the many ways in which the dominant attitudes and competitive behavior we have inherited threaten to push us dangerously out of balance with our world.

Our saving grace may be to use our awareness instead for tempering the silverback gorilla syndrome that has brought us success at such great cost. This book is an attempt to increase that awareness.

Western culture would have us remain oblivious to our primitive nature. Advertisers urge us to buy more running shoes so we can "be like Mike," and larger trucks so we can haul more stuff "like a rock." Healthcare practitioners furnish us with increasing doses of medication to subdue our aggressive tendencies and elevate our depressions. The heroes in our midst, however, portray another way to come to grips with our ancestry. Men such as Ralph Waldo Emerson, Mahatma Gandhi, Mikhail Gorbachev, and Martin Luther King all achieved a delicate dance by combining strength and passion with intuition and responsibility. We, too, can learn that dance, reach high with our aspirations, look deep within, and celebrate who we are—gorilla and all!

If you are a male reader who resonates with this evolutionary call, *great!* Share it, join a Silverback Gorilla 12-Step group, laugh, cry, find someone to eat lunch with.

But first be sure to make the acquaintance of . . .

Big G, the silverback gorilla,
lord of all he surveys,
leader of the pack,
top of the heap—
a specimen of power
and virility.

He possesses and rules all those around him.
A truly grand beast,
he is someone to be reckoned with,
not to be taken lightly —*even by himself* —
a commanding presence in any crowd.

3

But let's face it, Big G approaches every social situation with one of two questions:

#1   Fuck it?

#2 Kill it?

Although he may not act on these questions, they form the basis of his every meeting. Dominance is his prime directive.

The gender, clan, or age of each acquaintance determines which question Big G asks.

Welcoming home one of his "own" females, he assumes that she will respond positively to question #1.

He also assumes that she adores him and relies on him for protection.

He will give her a few opportunities to reject his advances before moving on to question #2.

Upon encountering an
unattached female,
Big G puffs up so she will see
what an obviously superior
gorilla he is . . .
leading again to question #1.

Immediately after meeting a female belonging
to another silverback, Big G automatically
advances to question #2,
hoping to eliminate the other male.

This way, Big G can take on the role of the female's
protector and eventually pose question #1.

If the female is too old,
way too young,
or for some reason undesirable,
Big G may decide
to let her hang around because,
after all, he is magnanimous

and she is a good bamboo-shoot washer,
banana peeler, or personal groomer,
showing potential for the future.

In Big G's view, babies—
often resulting from
the application of question #1—
are tolerable,

for they are a sign of his virility,
and after all,
the race must go on.

Upon encountering a male
who is competing for a mate—
or anything else, for that matter—
Big G goes directly to question #2.

He responds to the slightest challenging gesture
with put-downs and
attempts to dominate his foe.

If the male does not fall in line,
Big G takes immediate action.
The other creature is
shunned,
given demeaning work;
his position in the clan is ruined.

Worst of all,
he is made to look bad
in front of the females . . .

in which case he may wish he were dead.

If the other male is too young to compete,
our King of the Jungle may allow him to stay and serve,
offering to teach him how to be a gorilla.

The king is careful not to teach too much, however,
knowing the youngster will one day become a threat.

Big G knows that a certain number of these subordinates should be kept around for support in dealing with rivals.

An older male, too, may be endured,
allowed to stay and serve,
and occasionally consulted for advice.
His usefulness is limited in Big G's eyes,
but appearances must be kept up.

Power is the name of the game
for the silverback gorilla.

In a strategic moment
Big G may even approach another gorilla
with an expression of feelings,
or a suggestion of vulnerability.

With tears about
to flow from
his eyes,

he will drop hints about relationship difficulties.

Big G has discovered
that the appearance of vulnerability
can be employed as a power device.

Master of his world,
he would never request support,
however, and will automatically
reject any offer of help.

Because real vulnerability
would dissolve his image as leader
and inhibit his response to the prime directive,
Big G takes his sensitivity
and . . .

stuffs it.

He knows that if
as years go by
he slips a little,
he can always fall back on
experience,
  cunning,
    and bluffery

to maintain his self-image,

position,

personality,

and power.

Every now and then, an ambitious silverback
appears to win the game
and become
King of All the Jungles.

But does he really win
or must he just keep fighting?

Other silverbacks
spend their lives struggling,
never knowing the game
has no winners—

a dismal,
exhausting,
often life-threatening
charade to maintain.

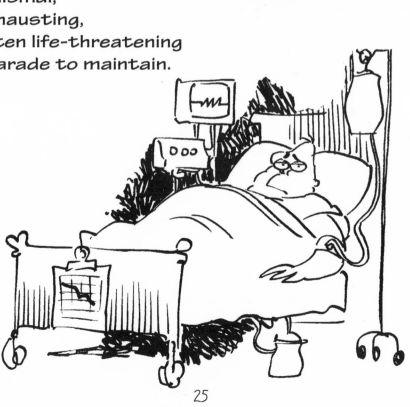

Yet Big G keeps it going,
in one way or another,

surrounding himself with
more and more symbols
that make him look powerful,

although *occasionally*
he suspects these
achievements are overrated.

Of course, real silverbacks
don't think about such issues.

They have never had the luxury of
self-evaluation.

Life works for them,
and they continue
to pass on their superior DNA.

Humans,
on the other hand,
are summoned to periods of introspection.

The call may come from without

or within.

It may knock gently on our door for years,

or come blasting through like a freight train.

We tend to react to this call with one of two D words:

denial . . .

or **depression.**

Or we may fight back,
defending gorilla behavior,

building entire religions around it,

taking refuge in the knowledge
that the game has been played this way
for thousands of years.

35

Fortunately,
awareness keeps calling
until we answer.

Our first response is to push Big G into the closet.

But even if we could succeed in stowing him away,

he would manage to escape
at the most inopportune times.

We then consider more permanent measures.

The truth is that the gorilla is too primal,
too powerful,
too central to our survival
to be eliminated.

Besides,
any attempt
to terminate him
is bound to fail.

Who *is* this guy called Big G?

He is raw and primal,
and lives in our guts.

He is passionate and excitable,
and lives in our hearts.

He is commanding yet simple,
fueling our imagination and creativity.

He is in charge of our physical existence
and rarely visits our heads;

it's much too complicated up there.

So why the denial,
the depression,
the trips to the closet,
the thoughts of extermination?

The problem is
that Big G has learned his role too well.

He has succeeded in dominating our world.

And the price we have paid is too steep

for our families,

our friends,

our coworkers,

our environment . . . and ourselves.

The challenge—
and any man with a gorilla in his gut
must be up for a challenge—
is to develop power within ourselves

while letting go of our need to dominate others.

We can start by examining all the ways in which
we exercise power over others:

we buy it,

we manipulate for it,

we bully for it,

EVICTION NOTICE... TAKE A HIKE!

we battle tooth and nail for it
as if our *lives* depended on it,

when in reality
only our *self-image*
is at stake.

Challenging the prime directive is not a job
to be tackled alone. Big G's support is needed.

But first we must assure him
of our desire for peaceful coexistence.

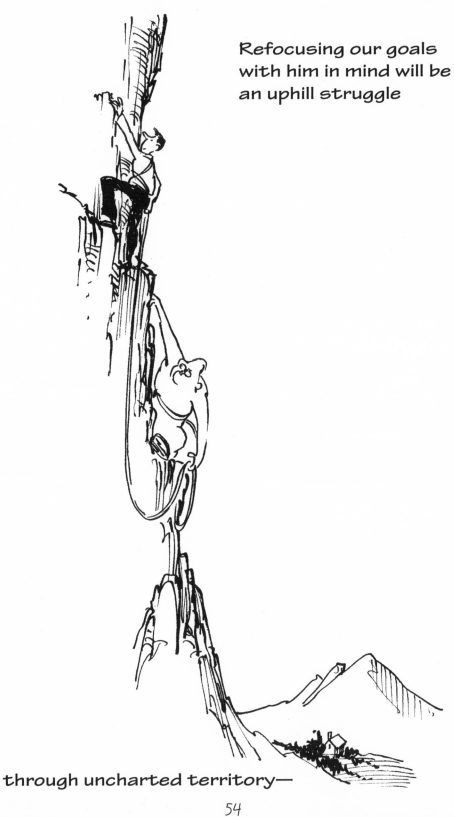

Refocusing our goals with him in mind will be an uphill struggle

through uncharted territory—

a trek perhaps more uncomfortable
than any we have undertaken.

But remember,
we are champions of discomfort,
and this journey
is worth each bead of sweat we give it.

Our first objective is to get to know the big guy—

to find out how he expresses himself,
what really turns him on,
how he feels while climbing a mountain
or signing a contract.

We will **discover** that he is always "on the make,"

that he loves to compete

and relishes a juicy challenge.

these are simply expressions of his passion for life.

We may not succeed in
getting to know him in a day,

a month,

or even a year.

But every step counts.

We will find that
our King of the Jungle needs a job,
a quest,

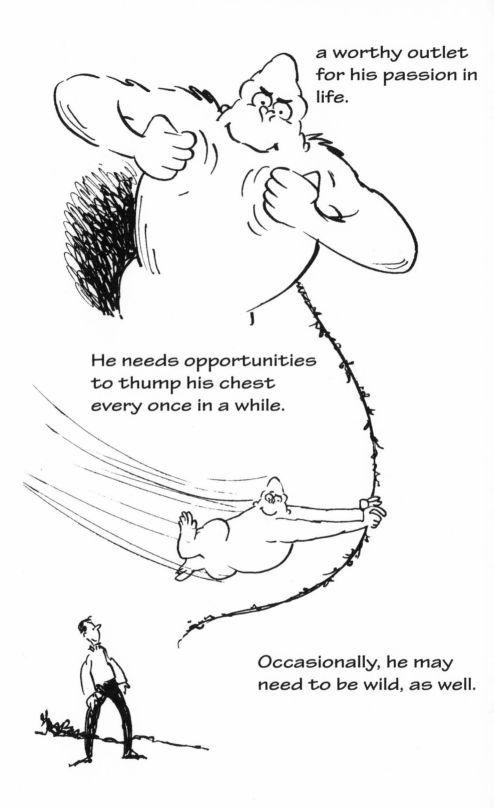

a worthy outlet for his passion in life.

He needs opportunities to thump his chest every once in a while.

Occasionally, he may need to be wild, as well.

Above all, he needs to experience joy!

This simple, primal emotion is
one a gorilla can hang his hat on.

Big G is a creature of
elementary feelings,

and in that sense
  he can teach *us* a thing or two,

provided that we slow down enough to listen,

see what really matters,

and find friends who will support our growth.

In time it will become clear
that we *both* need
to be needed,
to love and be loved,

to teach our young,
to pass on our enthusiasm for life

and to serve our community.

We will know we are on the right track
when we catch ourselves smiling
at odd moments,

when a former adversary asks for our help

or offers support,

when the tension is released in our chest and guts,

when we laugh inappropriately,

when we let a challenge pass us by.

We will know we are on the right track
when a female
is simply honored and admired,

when we are willing to look into the darkness

we've been avoiding all these years.

We'll know we are on the right track
when "service" becomes a priority—

not out of a need to help
or rescue,
but because
it feels
good
inside.

These signs are subtle,
unlike the brassy affirmations we are used to.

To identify them,
we will have to listen deeply
to our hearts

and risk being expressive,

no matter how different
our passions may be
from those of our peers.

Each time we express ourselves,
we will become more
of who we really are . . .

until secure in our magnificence,
we will be able to celebrate
magnificence in others.

About the Contributors

Jeff Hood, an organizational consultant, has a master's degree in counseling and is passionately involved in training men, women, and teens to be more respectful and celebratory of life. He also facilitates outdoor community-building experiences in the great American wilderness. He has sat in steamy sweat lodges, rolled in river mud, roared from mountaintops, and guided rafts through the Grand Canyon. By the grace of God, he has discovered Big J out in the wild where there is still room to rumble. Jeff has been married, survived a divorce, and raised two children. As for Big , he drives a 1972 MGB and parks his sailboat in the yard.

Jack Lindstrom, at an early age, resisted all efforts to do anything worthwhile and chose instead a life of cartooning. Armed with a BFA from the Minneapolis College of Art and Design and a desire to show people that life "ain't all that serious," he has pursued a career doing light illustration for the print media. With William Wells, he produces a syndicated comic strip called "Executive Suite" for the United Features Syndicate.

Jack has been married for over forty years to his high chool sweetheart. He spends his hours away from the drawing board exposing is three grandchildren to the wonders of golf.

Order Form

Quantity   Amount

_____   *The Silverback Gorilla Syndrome: Transforming*
         Primitive Man ($12.00)   _____

                    Sales tax of 6.25% (New Mexico residents)   _____

                    Shipping and handling (see chart below)   _____

                             Total amount enclosed   _____

Quantity discounts available

Shipping and handling		
<u>Surface</u>	<u>First Class</u>	plus $1.00 per book
$2.70	$4.00	on orders of 2 or more

Method of payment

☐ Check or money order enclosed (made payable to **Adventures in Spirit Publications** in US currency only)

☐ MasterCard   _ _ _ _ - _ _ _ _ - _ _ _ _ - _ _ _ _

☐ VISA   Expiration date   _ _ _ _

         Signature _____

Please photocopy this order form, fill it out, and mail it, together with your personal check, money order, or charge-card information, to:

Adventures in Spirit Publications
PO Box 6096
Santa Fe, NM 87502
800-729-4692